GW00541125

Dundee
in old picture postcards volume 2

Norman Watson

European Library   ZALTBOMMEL/THE NETHERLANDS

Cover picture:

Dundee's much-loved and sadly-lost Wellgate Steps. See picture 1.

Acknowledgements:

I am grateful to those who assisted in the production of this volume, notably to D.C. Thomson and Co. for their assistance and also to Shirley Blair of that company for her help in preparing the text. In particular I would like to thank Mr. Bill Early for his kindness in lending several fine early cards.

The author:

Dr. Norman Watson is a journalist with The Courier in Dundee, for which he writes news and current affairs features. He is the author of several books, including *Perth in old picture postcards* volume 1 and volume 2 and *Dundee in old picture postcards* volume 1 for the European Library, the Netherlands. He lectures on a part-time basis on media issues and aspects of history.

BACK IN TIME

GB ISBN 90 288 6682 5

© 2001 European Library – Zaltbommel/The Netherlands

European Library
post office box 49
NL – 5300 AA Zaltbommel/The Netherlands
telephone: 0031 418 513144
fax: 0031 418 515515
e-mail: publisher@eurobib.nl

Introduction

Since the first volume *Dundee in old picture postcards* was published in 1997, the city and its environs have undergone far-reaching change. This is no better illustrated in the first instance than by charting its transforming physical appearance. Dundee's world-class reputation as a centre for scientific research, for example, has been enhanced by the opening of the £12 million Wellcome Trust research centre on Hawkhill, and through NCR's decision to site a major research and development factory on Kingsway West to reinforce its position as one of the world's leading producers of automated teller machines.

Technology Park, on the city's western outskirts, has continued to harness sustainable inward investment opportunities, and major call centres for BT, Norwich Union and the Bank of Scotland complement emerging strengths in creative industries on this important development site. Elsewhere, a city-wide campaign to win Civil Service jobs has led to three government agencies being sited in Dundee.

The stunning £250 million new Overgate shopping centre, building on a £26 million redevelopment of the Wellgate centre, has led the way in the reinvigoration of Dundee's commercial heart, to the extent that Dundee city centre was named UK Town Centre of the Year in 1999. These developments are now enhanced by a mix of new businesses and retail outlets at the innovative City Quay complex.

Since the publication of volume 1, Dundee has also enjoyed a growing reputation as one of the country's centres of educational excellence. Now with two universities, the student population reaches 26,000 during term time, with 4,000 graduates every year, and the sector remains one of the biggest influences and contributors to life in the city.

Culturally, the opening of Dundee Contemporary Arts in 1999 transformed the Perth Road area. Along with the ever-popular Dundee Rep theatre and the new Sensation science centre nearby, DCA forms a triangle of popular attractions now regarded as the city's Cultural Quarter.

Leisure provision has also been improved through the opening of Dundee Ice Arena on the city's western outskirts. Recently Dundee has planned a 30,000 capacity dual-use stadium at Caird Park as part of Scotland's bid to host the Euro 2008 football competition.

Elsewhere, Captain Scott's polar research ship Discovery, an icon of Britain's pioneering past, remains a totem of the city's future dynamism. In many respects the city has rediscovered itself since the ship's arrival in 1986. Boasting the award-winning Discovery Point, home to RRS Discovery, and Verdant Works, the 1999 European Museum of the Year, Dundee attracts some 570,000 visitors every year to its multifarious visitor attractions.

Dundee, then, has undergone a period of reinvention, increasing confidence and discovery, and gradually receding are the problems with image created through misjudgements on the city, which have dogged it since the era of jute dominance.

So to the postcards and photographs of volume 2. The constant theme is to show scenes that will rekindle memories for those familiar with Dundee, and create interest among those yet to discover the city. Mostly, the postcards come from the Edwardian period, the 'Golden Era' when up to 900 million cards were posted annually.

What, I think, they serve to show collectively is that while Dundee may have been a one-industry town for a few decades either side of 1900, the photographic record of that period points to a fine city, which boasted a harbour by Thomas Telford, an Adam town house, a library by the 'greatest Victorian architect' and a park designed by the pre-eminent British landscape engineer.

Its civic heart was beating strongly, it was largely comfortable with many aspects of its appearance, and its people regarded it with pride.

1 Steeped in local folk-lore, the famous Wellgate Steps linked Murraygate and Hilltown by crossing Victoria Road. The regeneration of the east end of the city centre, particularly the creation of the Wellgate shopping centre in 1977, led to the historic passageway being closed. The steps are seen here in a locally-produced J.B. White postcard from about 1925.

THE WELLGATE STEPS, DUNDEE.

2   Alex Johnston's shop at the junction of Perth Road and Seafield Road would be regarded as an upmarket delicatessen nowadays. When this picture was taken around 1910, it was one of a number of Johnston grocery and provision stores in Dundee stocking a huge range of cheeses, hams and other domestic necessities – such as Bovril! In Victorian times, stores would often open late to catch trade after the closure of the city's public houses. This meant long hours for the staff, with some female assistants in licensed grocers working an estimated 90 hours a week – much more than a mill worker.

3 This fine study of Stewart Street, off Lorne Street, shows life in Lochee before the modern Dundee suburb emerged. Scenes of tenements, horse-drawn carts, cobbled streets and barefooted bairns rekindle memories of a more tranquil time, but conceal desperately difficult days for so many disadvantaged families in Dundee's socalled 'Tipperary' district, where overcrowding and poor sanitation was a way of life. Lochee was absorbed into the burgh of Dundee in 1859.

4   Dundee suffragettes were at the forefront of the struggle for women's votes in the Edwardian period of heightened militancy. Scotland's first votes-for-women protest took place in the city. The first women imprisoned in Scotland were jailed in Dundee and the first hunger strikes were adopted in the city. Ethel Moorhead, Scotland's most notorious militant suffragette, was a Dundee woman, while some of the worst outrages, protests and violent actions took place in the city. Here we see the suffrage women recruiting for a meeting at Foresters' Halls, Nicoll Street, in 1908.

5   Postmarked Broughty Ferry in 1911 this card is thought to show the pioneering mothers' and babies' restaurant opened by Dundee Social Union in 1906, the first in the country. The restaurant charged tuppence (1p) for dinner, but allowed deserving cases free food. Its objectives were to encourage breast feeding of infants and to discourage mothers working in Dundee's mills and factories. The restaurant superintendents, one of whom can possibly be seen on the left, gave mothers advice on baby care and arranged some 1,000 home visits a year by 1909.

6 A firm surviving from the Edwardian era is Robert Curr and Dewar, the city centre auctioneers. Here we see Robert Curr's Dundee Auction Rooms in Ward Road around the 1880s. An article in The Dundee Advertiser in August 1909 (at the height of suffrage militancy in the city!) was far from politically correct when it claimed that the auctioneer's profession was 'threatened by a feminine invasion' of women auctioneers: 'Clearly in this sphere women will not do,' it concluded! Brave talk – the previous census had shown there were 17,421 more women than men over the age of 20 in Dundee!

7   Sailing ships line astern in Victoria Dock towards the end of the 19th century rekindle recent memories of the visit to the same dockside area in 2001 of four visiting vessels from the Tall Ships' Race. Dundee's docks were largely due to the design brilliance of the civil engineer Thomas Telford, who laid out the West Graving Dock in 1823. King William IV Dock opened two years later in front of 20,000 spectators. Earl Grey Dock was completed in 1834.

8   The apparently well-stocked Royal Arch Tea-room was located in Dock Street and from the faint reflections of ships' masts in the right-hand window of this 'shop-front' post-card, it can be assumed that it overlooked the docks themselves. Note the large advertisements for Fry's Chocolate – whose in-house advertising post-cards change hands now-adays for considerable sums.

9   Advertisements also dominate this circa 1905 photograph of South Union Street. Everything from Perth Dye Works to His Majesty's Theatre, Hudson's Soap and Oxo are placed before passers-by, while, to the left, the familiar sight of Downie's Dining Rooms provide mouth-watering memories of the days of shilling dinners! Local prices around 1915 were: eggs, 2s 8d a dozen (13p), butter 3s a pound (15p) and rice 7d a pound (3p).

10 Next to a postcard
from 1914 and the
celebrations marking the
royal visit of King George
V and Queen Mary to
Dundee in July that year.
Here we see the royal party
crossing High Street.
The entrance to Keiller's
factory nearby was trans-
formed into a magnificent
floral arch, behind which
five hundred employees
and former employees of
the marmalade family
dynasty, all immaculately
turned out in white
overalls, waited to greet
the visitors.

Royal Procession crossing High Street,
Dundee, July 1914.

11 The visit of another queen – Queen Victoria in 1844 – was commemorated by the hurried building of a precarious wooden arch at her point of arrival in Dock Street. Six years later the Royal Arch was replaced with an identical structure in sandstone (seen here about 1900), but in 1964 it was pulled down to make way for the construction of the Tay Road Bridge landfall area. Note the long ladder, right foreground, for lighting inspections and repairs.

12   In 1907 Lt Ernest Shackleton set out in the former Dundee whaler Nimrod to achieve 'furthest south'. The great polar explorer had strong links with the city. He stood for election as a Unionist (Conservative) parliamentary candidate in 1906, finishing fourth, and in 1914 he was astounded to discover that the Dundee jute magnate Sir James Caird was prepared to fund his Trans-Antarctic expedition to the tune of £23,000 – several millions in today's terms.

13 It was another great Dundee ship, the Terra Nova, which secured Captain Scott's place in history by carrying him on his ill-fated voyage towards the South Pole in 1910 – from which he was not to return. Here we see the Terra Nova on a commemorative postcard of 1912, with 'The late Capt Scott' inset. The Terra Nova was the last steam whaler built in Dundee (in 1884) and the last ship built by the famous Stephen's yard.

CAPT. SCOTT'S SHIP THE "TERRA NOVA".

The South Pole Hero.

The Late Capt. Scott.

14 Isn't this a heart-warming scene of a by-gone age – small boys with pond yachts, girls feeding swans – in the tranquil setting of Stobsmuir Ponds? But, come winter, every Dundee lad seemed to know when it was time to get the ice skates out for the frozen Stobbie! The scene has hardly changed down passing decades, though today's swans are presumably the several-times great grandsons of those pictured here!

STOBSMUIR PONDS, DUNDEE.

15 This is an unusual sight – workmen laying the foundation stone of the Caird Hall in June 1914. Read the wording on the stone today and an explanation is forthcoming – the formal laying of the foundation stone took place the following month and was achieved 'miraculously' by King George V by electrical connection during a visit to Sir James Caird's Ashton jute works in Hawkhill.

16 This fine study from the 1920s shows Castle Lane, which ran from Castle Court in Castle Street. The photographer is positioned close to the entrance of the Criterion Bar. The Greenmarket runs off to the right. Three polls at three-year intervals in the 1920s allowed Dundee citizens to decide whether they wanted to rid the city of its hard-drinking image by closing down or limiting the opening of its pubs. They were offered No Change, No Licence or Limitation of the licence. On all three occasions the vote was for No Change!

17   Now to a busy Edwardian view of the West Port. This picture conveys why, even today, the West Port retains a strong identity of its own. Once it was a separate suburb, only absorbed into Dundee as a result of protracted negotiations – sometimes over drawn swords! Formerly a warren of tenements, it is now the focal point for regenerated housing, small individual shops and a prodigious student population.

Nest Port, Dundee   Valentines Serie

18 Dundee's hard-drinking reputation (it had 389 public houses in 1920!) was probably not enhanced by the presence of two pubs 'cheek by jowl' in the Hilltown – seen here on a R.H. Lundie card postmarked 1911. Note the absence of tramlines in the picture. The 'foot' of the Hilltown, as this card is captioned, was too steep for the trams. The peak year for trams was 1932, when 79 tramways were in operation in the city.

FOOT OF HILLTOWN, DUNDEE.

ELCO SERIES

19   Now we are at the West Port looking up Hawkhill on a Valentine's Series postcard from the early 1900s. Note again the busy comings and go-ings and rattling trams in this working-class city en-clave. During Communist-led riots here in September 1921, windows were smashed with missiles commandeered from broken 'cassies' and mounted police had to form a line to prevent looting.

20 This unusual photograph from 1954 shows the large sundial, which was located in the vicinity of Dock Street. Known as Dundee Harbour sundial, it was dismantled and removed during preparatory work for the new road bridge. However invaluable a sundial might be as a chronometer, they could only be of use in daylight and when the sun was shining. One wonders why Dundee had one in the first place, then!

21 The Communist Party has enjoyed a prominent position on Dundee's political map. The city, for example, has put forward as many Communist candidates for general elections as anywhere in the UK, including Willie Gallacher, who stood against both Winston Churchill and the Temperance leader Edwin Scrymgeour in 1922. Here a Communist Party May Day march in the 1950s ends in City Square. Note the prominent 'Stop the drive to War' message to the superpower rivals.

22 Taken before 1900, this photograph looks east along the Nethergate towards the High Street. The building in the foreground, right, is St. Andrew's Roman Catholic Cathedral. To the left is Tay Street. Approaching in the centre is a curious steam tram from the 1880s. In the mid-1990s, the eminent Scottish historian Emeritus Professor A.A. Duncan of Glasgow University delivered a paper to the Abertay Historical Society in which he asserted that Dundee was first established in the Nethergate area, rather than the more commonly held Seagate.

23 One of a set of 12 Blind School postcards issued by the Simmath Press, Perth Road, around 1920, the top section of this divided card shows a mixed class of 14 pupils. The lower section shows the pupils taking part in dancing instruction. Dundee Institute for the Blind was opened in Magdalens Green in 1885. It benefited from electric power in 1912, and from a visit from King George V two years later.

A CLASSROOM.

DANCING LESSONS, DUNDEE BLIND INSTITUTION.

24 The Mars Training Ship was a familiar sight in the Tay between 1869, when it arrived, and 1929 when it was towed to Inverkeithing to be scrapped. The Mars was home to some 6,500 boys during its 60-year stay on the Tay. Its original purpose was quite different, however. It was built at Chatham in the 1840s as an 81-gun, four-deck man o' war!

Training Ship, "Mars," on the River Tay.

25 The city-centre publishing offices of D.C. Thomson & Co. in Meadowside are seen here under construction in 1901. Built from Dumfries sandstone and known as Courier Buildings, the offices were opened in 1911 and were added to by a tower block in 1960. Sculptures of Literature and Justice feature above the impressive side entrance.

26 Photographed from an unusual angle is the architectural glory of Sir George Gilbert Scott's Albert Institute. The site in Meadowside had previously been occupied by a miscellaneous assortment of sheds and booths, which the civic fathers agreed were 'quite unsuited for its central position in a thriving city'. But the institute's construction in honour of Prince Albert, who died in 1861, was difficult because it was to be erected upon reclaimed ground that filled the bed of the diverted Scouring burn, which ran through the meadows. The problems of foundations were eventually overcome by resting the structure upon massive oak piles.

27   Now we travel along the coast to the suburb of Broughty Ferry, which was controversially 'dragged screaming and kicking' into Dundee in 1913, after a lengthy and acrimonious debate.

Seventy-five years earlier the Dundee-Arbroath Railway had brought overnight prosperity to the sleepy suburb – allowing the Dundee managerial classes to escape from a city, which they perceived to be riddled with health risks.

Here we see a water cart passing under the low railway bridge at the eastern end of Brook Street.

28 Broughty Ferry owed its existence to its position to defend the Tay estuary, and a castle was built on the rocky promontory commanding control of the mile-wide channel. The fishermen's cottages, which evolved around the castle, developed into a community largely in-dependent from Dundee, three miles distant.
This splendid study shows the smaller boats and the fishermen's cottages along the shoreline in the 1890s. The lifeboat shed, the subject of a controversial extension in 2001, is seen in the background.

29 Here, the men of the Ferry prepare for their fishing duties, while an east coast breeze has encouraged their womenfolk to take advantage of good drying weather.

30 A postcard dated June 1910 shows a clutch of submarines at the Naval Base, Dundee. There was great excitement in The Courier during 1908 and 1909 as first news of the new base, and then its newly-won role and strategic importance, was revealed to readers. Dundee was also a major centre of submarine activity in the Second World War, when a multi-national fleet of twenty vessels tied up at King George Wharf.

SUBMARINES AT NAVAL BASE, DUNDEE.

31 This fine study of Tally Street in old Dundee shows the City Hotel on the left, which later became the New Imperial Hotel. Next to it is the original outlet of Wilkie the butcher's, and then the familiar commercial frontage of Robertson's house furnishers.

32 Like Dundee's submarines, HMS Unicorn was built for war, but never fired a shell in anger. Now one of the oldest warships still afloat in the world and a familiar sight on the Tay since 1873, the Unicorn has been cared for by the Unicorn Preservation Society since 1968 and is open to the public.

H. M. S. "Unicorn", Dundee

33 Part of the Admiral's series of Edwardian postcards featured the great Dundee naval hero Adam Duncan (1731-1804). As Admiral Duncan he led the British fleet to victory over the Dutch at the Battle of Camperdown in 1797, thereby averting a possible invasion of Britain. Elevated to the peerage as a reward from a grateful nation, he took the title Viscount Duncan of Camperdown. A campaign is currently underway to turn Camperdown House into a maritime museum.

34 A railway disaster sends an excited newspaper boy off and running from the back of Courier Buildings in Euclid Crescent. Turn-of-the-century paperboys could earn one shilling (5p) a week and were expected to deliver their Couriers by quarter to six in the morning. The Courier cost only a penny at the time – but more often than not, they were passed round half a tenement!

35   Here is a sight to gladden the heart of hungry Dundonians the world over! Wallace's Auld Dundee Pie Shop was a fixture in the town. The branch seen here was located in the Vault, a narrow passage that ran behind William Adam's Town House of 1731. The cramped housing in this area once produced some of the highest levels of disease and mortality in Scotland.

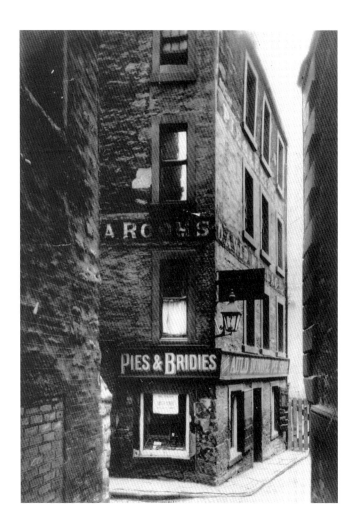

36   Now a move to the Cowgate and a splendid advertising postcard from about 1910 showing Alexander McHardy's People's Pharmacy. The poster on the left-hand window advertises Cod Liver Oil, while the large poster on the right encourages shoppers to try Wood's Cough Emulsion – 'The Reliable Cough Cure' – available in two sizes at 1/- or 1/9d.

37 The most momentous civic event of 1914 was the visit to Dundee of King George V and Queen Mary. Here we see preparations for the royal procession in Whitehall Street, with garlands of flowers and some rather rigid-looking crowd barriers! The street later became best-known for Draffen's department store, which became Debenhams in the early 1980s.

38 This Edwardian-era postcard shows a general view of the stage and proscenium of Green's Playhouse in the Nethergate. Green's steel, glass and concrete art deco tower became a prominent feature of Dundee after its completion in 1936. But the tower had to be hauled down as part of demolition work after the former cinema was destroyed by fire in 1995. Two years later, however, the fondly-remembered feature of the Dundee city centre skyline rose from the ashes as part of the £8 million redevelopment of the site as a 2000-seat Mecca bingo hall.

GENERAL VIEW OF STAGE & PROSCENIUM, GREENS PLAYHOUSE, NETHERGATE, DUNDEE.

39 Now back to Broughty Ferry, and a George Washington Wilson postcard showing two young lads making a dash to catch the Monifieth-bound tram whizzing along Queen Street behind them. Did they catch it? We'll never know. Or perhaps they were simply daring to run in front of it – as some nerveless kids do in today's traffic! The Ferry's grid-iron street plan was set out in the 19th century by Charles Hunter of Burnside and included St. Vincent Street and Fort Street, names associated with British victories during the Napoleonic Wars.

40 Tons of sand pile up on the front at Broughty Ferry after high winds in 1959. No need of ices or refreshing lemonade that day! In 1873 there were 35 places in the Ferry for the retail of drink – more per head of population than in any other village in Scotland. Perhaps this was further inducement to potential holidaymakers!

41 Queen Alexandra, wife of King Edward VII, visited Dundee briefly in 1907 and 1908, after spending the summer at Balmoral. Here, bailies and civic dignitaries prepare to speed her on her way by pinnace to the royal yacht, as she bids goodbye to Lord Provost William Longair. On both occasions the Queen was on her way to Norway to visit relations. She was the eldest daughter of King Christian IX of Denmark.

Queen's Visit to Dundee — Her Majesty bids Good-bye to Lord Provost Longair

42   One of the strangest acts ever seen at the Palace Theatre in Nethergate (seen here in the 1930s) was a huge Frenchman who was billed as the Human Aquarium. A large tank of water containing assorted fish was placed on the stage. He proceeded to scoop up the fish with a jug and to swallow them. He would then take a stance several yards away and with one glorious belch, his 'prisoners' would be released to cascade back into the tank! The Palace was built in 1870 for use both as a theatre and a circus. The original circus ring was discovered during its later conversion into a cinema.

43   Parts of the famous Kinnaird Hall can still be seen in Bank Street. Alas, few photographs of what must have been an impressive interior appear to have survived. This remarkable poster shows the programme of events in the hall in April 1893, when the Rosicrucian somnomists Professor S.S. Baldwin and his wife Kitie, on their 'fourth tour around the globe... a gigantic success everywhere' presented 'the queerest and quaintest, the funniest show on earth'. In short, they were hypnotists!

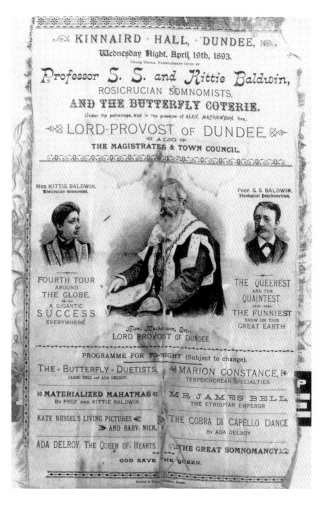

44 As postcard production became more sophisticated publishers astutely concluded that they could 'lengthen the life' of commissioned photographs by including them in composite cards. Here, a Good Luck From Dundee card by Valentine's uses scenes featured on postcards some years earlier. Fascinatingly, the sender in June 1956 writes: 'Shops very busy. TV is a great attraction.'

THE CITY SQUARE

GOOD LUCK FROM DUNDEE

TAY BRIDGE FROM N.

RIVERSIDE DRIVE

NETHERGATE AND OLD STEEPLE

45   Similarly, a photograph's 'life' could be extended by its incorporation within a decorative border. This postcard shows Dundee's Royal Arch contained within a Fraser tartan border, and formed part of Hartmann's Glossy Tartan Series of 1910. A very rare Cynicus postcard is known with a view of Dundee within a border made from tartan material. Jute and aluminium Dundee cards are also recorded.

46   Comic postcards were instantly popular when they emerged in the early Edwardian period – and the sauciest seaside types remained so for the rest of the century! 'This is the way you get your shave,' writes a squaddie from Barry Camp to his brother in High Blantyre.

Barry Camp, on the Dundee-Arbroath road, was one of the first militia and volunteer camps established in the 19th century as a result of the fear of war with France.

47   The Red Cross Auxiliary Hospital in Broughty Ferry provided forty beds for wounded servicemen during the Great War. In 1965 the legendary amputee air ace Douglas Bader opened Dundee Limb Fitting Centre in the building. The development of the centre proved a model for the care of amputees and, before its services were relocated to Ninewells in 1999, more than 3,000 patients passed through its doors, with the vast majority being successfully fitted with artificial limbs and returning home.

RED CROSS AUXILIARY HOSPITAL, THE LODGE, BROUGHTY FERRY

48 The sight of the un-adorned Tay Ferries booking office, seen here in the summer of 1952, will evoke nostalgic memories for those who miss the famous 'Fifies'. Newport developed primarily due to the presence of the ferry. But while the service passed into the pages of local history in 1966, Newport continued to prosper as an important and well-to-do dormitory town.

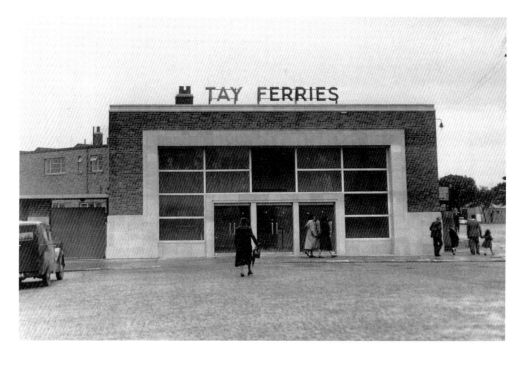

49 We now see heavy goods vehicles waiting to load on to the ferries in 1957. The Scotscraig ferry, constructed in 1951 by the Caledon Yard in Dundee, made the last ferry crossing on 18 August 1966, with the newly-constructed road bridge in full view of her passengers. Despite that historic role the Scotscraig was quickly sold on and spent the last years of her useful life in Malta.

50 The hall seen on the right of this photograph should also invoke happy memories among those who joined the Sea Cadets as young lads in the 1950s and early 1960s.
The building near the Royal Arch was used as the headquarters of the Dundee unit of the Sea Cadets' Corps until 1963, when it was demolished to make room for the approach roads of the Tay Road Bridge.

51 Back to the city centre, and a scene similar to that shown in picture 22 of the Nethergate from the Queen's Hotel. St. Andrew's Roman Catholic Cathedral can be seen on the right, while the West Park electric tram is passing the site of today's hugely-popular Dundee Contemporary Arts centre.

The Nethergate, from the Queen's Hotel, Dundee.

52 Thomas Telford's Craig Pier is seen in this lovely postmarked card of 1906, which uses a photograph taken in 1893 showing the paddle steamer Dundee about to berth.

'This doesn't look a very good day to sail,' says the sender to a Mrs. Rennie in Broughty Ferry in a gentle snapshot of Edwardian life. 'We can meet in the arcade and have a sail another day.' The card is posted at 11.30 a.m., arranging to meet at 2 p.m. that day. What faith in the postal system!

53   So now we see D.M. Brown's Arcade in the Murraygate in a Tuck's Glosso series postcard from around 1910. Parts of the Murraygate were redeveloped as a result of the Improvement Act of 1871, when some of its most densely-populated areas – where child mortality rates were commonly 40 per thousand, compared to 5 per thousand live births today – were pulled down.

DUNDEE. MURRAYGATE.

54 The 551 ft bare summit of the Law rises serenely above expanding Dundee in this postcard from the first years of the 20th century. It is the highest point within city boundaries and, somewhat naturally, it has been fortified since the Iron Age at least. Much of the housing around the Law – notably the Lawton estate itself – came about as a result of inter-war housing development under the provisions of the 1924 Housing Act.

The Law, Dundee.

55 Dundee's proudly-prominent war memorial, set on the top of the Law, originally commemorated those who fell in the Great War. General Sir Ian Hamilton unveiled it on 16 May 1925.
The memorial's beacon is illuminated four times a year, most notably on Remembrance Day each November.

War Memorial, Law Hill, Dundee

56 This splendid Edwardian postcard by Davidson Brothers shows children parading their Easter bonnets in front of the pavilion in Baxter Park. Dundee's only formal Victorian park, Baxter Park, was a gift to the city by Sir David Baxter, who employed the great landscape engineer Joseph Paxton – the architect of the Crystal Palace – to advise on its design. Seventy thousand people attended its opening in 1863.

Series 5027 . J   BAXTER PARK. DUNDEE.   Davidson Brothers
LONDON

57 Logie housing estate, beneath Balgay Hill, was the first municipal housing scheme in Scotland and was laid out in 1919 by James Thomson, the city's town architect and engineer. Thomson is also credited with the creation of Britain's first 'ring road' at Kingsway, which was originally meant to bypass the city, but now forms a vital traffic artery.

LOGIE (FIRST HOUSING SCHEME IN SCOTLAND) DUNDEE.

58 Dundee's time gun never stood the test of time. Seen here on a hand-coloured card postmarked September 1912, the gun was situated at Dudhope Castle and fired daily at one o' clock. Alas its booming 'voice' caused distress among wounded servicemen at Dundee Royal Infirmary nearby and the gun was withdrawn from daily service in 1916. There were moves in 1924 to have it reinstated, but councillors argued successfully that the Barrack Park gun used to be heard from 'Lochee to Broughty Ferry' and that their lives shouldn't have to be regulated by such noise!

The Time Gun
Dundee

59 'Samuel's Corner' on this stylish card clearly identifies Reform Street. The Reform Act of 1832 gave the street its name. In November 1832 a public notice in The Courier alluded to a different kind of reform – 'A public meeting will be held in the Steeple Church on Friday evening, for the purpose of forming an Anti-Slavery Society for Dundee. Those who are friendly to the entire and immediate abolition of slavery in the Colonies and Dependencies of Great Britain are invited to attend.'
One wonders what became of it?

Reform Street, Dundee

60   Car No 36 making its way to West Park in June 1956 passes another notable 'corner' meeting place – G.L. Wilson's – known to all in Dundee as 'The Corner'. Garnet Wilson, one of the Wilson family of drapery store proprietors, was Lord Provost of Dundee during the Second World War. The store closed in 1971.

61 To the Nethergate next, and firstly to a very fine card from February 1919 in which the sender writes: 'They have an overseas club here for troops on leave.' Then he adds negatively: 'I think they could have found a better town. It is very cold and misty all of the time.' It is well we can focus on the card's terrific front!

Nethergate Looking East, DUNDEE

62   Now a 1930s' summer view of the City Churches area in the Nethergate, with motor cars beginning to have a considerable presence. The Royal Hotel on the right survived until recent times and now provides a mix of accommodation. In 1904, the first Dundee car registration TS 1 was given to a Mr. Thomas Shaw, who had a bicycle dealership in Whitehall Street.

Nethergate, Dundee.

63 We move east now to Brook Street, Broughty Ferry, which was formed after a feuing arrangement was drawn up, which incorporated its older buildings and which made provision for the buildings we see today. Broughty Ferry became a fashionable seaside resort when the railways arrived in 1839.

64 August 1954 must have produced the odd swelter of a day if this happy scene of Broughty Ferry beach is anything to go by. A long-gone bathing shelter is seen on the left. Presumably the hard-working dermatologists at Ninewells Hospital will recognize with some regret the days when headgear for children wasn't a seaside pre-requisite along with bucket and spade!

65　This fine Adelphi Series card is postmarked 1918 and shows how Victoria Road was very much a highly-populated and busy thoroughfare in working class Dundee, and an important thoroughfare linking major jute works and the docks. Although much of 'Victorian' Victoria Road has been lost to development, some of the mills and factories remain to this day, particularly A. & S. Hendry's fine jute finishing works of 1874-1875.

66 Postcards of Dundee's suburbs are always highly prized, not just as collectors' items but as a means of charting the city's development. This rare card from 1936 shows Noran Avenue in Craigiebank. The sender, a resident of Gannochie Terrace, which shares a junction with Noran Avenue, writes: 'Hello Canada! This is me home again!' Craigiebank was part of the drive towards high-quality four-in-a-block housing in Dundee in the inter-war years, with rents pitched not for the working class, but for 'skilled artisans and white collar workers'.

NORAN AVENUE, CRAIGIEBANK, DUNDEE.

67   Here we look up St. Andrew's Street towards St. Andrew's Church, which, dating from 1772, is not only the oldest surviving church in Dundee, but also the only Trades kirk in Scotland. The buildings in the right foreground were removed to allow for the road system adjacent to Dundee's bus station. The tenement top left eventually made way for the construction of the Wellgate centre. Fittingly we see three horse-drawn carts passing Robert Sim's saddler's shop.

896   ST. ANDREWS STREET, DUNDEE   VALENTINES SERIES

68 How splendid the Angus Hotel must have seemed as an example of state-of-the-art concrete technology in the early 1960s – and a few years before a much larger demonstration of its properties came along in the form of the Tay Bridge! Note the once-familiar Andrew G. Kidd delivery van passing the hotel entrance.

69 Dundee fishwives form a delightful subject for the Raphael Tuck & Son photographer. The fish-wives gathered in the Greenmarket area three times a week to sell from their baskets. Sometimes the 'wives' came from Arbroath – by foot! One of Tuck's Oilette series, the caption on the card reads: 'Early Morning Dundee Market – Waiting for Buyers!'

EARLY MORNING
DUNDEE MARKET
"WAITING FOR BUYERS."

"Oilette"

70 Popularly known as 'Doc Stewart's', the Downfield Tavern in Strathmartine Road is seen in this rare postcard from the early 20th century. The semi-detached villas which categorize the suburb of Downfield today, were established for the relatively well-off in the last decades of the 19th century. Despite the fortunes, which many of Dundee's mill owners amassed, it has been estimated that £5 million of investment – equivalent to around £200 million today – flowed westwards to various business ventures in the United States – in the 1870s alone!

TAVERN, DOWNFIELD. Phone : 171

71 Watson Street and Ferry Road formed an important peripheral junction 100 years ago. This fine postcard shows a tram well on its way to Monifieth and passing a wonderful sweep of terraced housing. Dundee's first tramway was established in 1877 and ran along Perth Road to Blackness Toll.

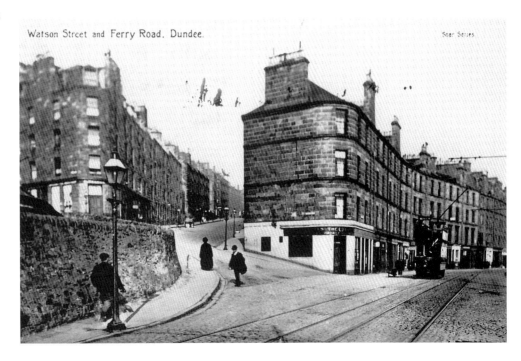

Watson Street and Ferry Road, Dundee.

Star Series

72 The Central Hotel occupied the corner site on the junction of Ward Road and Court House Square and is seen on a locally-published J.B. White card. The hotel site is now occupied by offices, but the Palladian-style courthouse, which included the police office and jail when constructed in 1833, has undergone recent refurbishment and continues its original judicial function.

Central Hotel, Dundee.

73 David Small's delicate watercolours of his home city were snapped up by the famous postcard publisher Raphael Tuck for a memorable early series of Dundee 'Oilette' cards. Small (1846-1927) was a popular local illustrator, and his original watercolours now fetch handsome prices in salerooms. Here we see his depiction of High Street in 1904 with Dundee's ill-fated, much-missed Town House prominent on the right.

High Street, Dundee

74　In 1901 American-based multi-millionaire Andrew Carnegie gave Dundee £37,000 for the supply of four branch libraries and a central reading room upon sites which would be provided by local citizens. The Arthurstone, Blackness, Coldside (seen here about 1910) and St. Roque's branch libraries, and the central reading rooms at Ward Road (which later became Barrack Street museum) duly opened between the years 1905 and 1911.

COLDSIDE LIBRARY, DUNDEE

75 Look up to roof-level at the bottom of Whitehall Street and a reminder of one of Dundee's most popular Victorian hotels can be seen in the form of the wording 'Mathers Hotel' on a gable end. Mathers Temperance Hotel was built in 1900 and remained 'dry' for the following 69 years, when it became the Tay Centre Hotel. Mathers was frequently used by stars appearing in celebrity concerts in the Caird Hall. In 1941, however, it was requisitioned by the Royal Navy and its fine views over the estuary were obscured by the black cloth nailed over its windows.

MATHERS HOTEL, DUNDEE.   B.1625.

76 Finally, we see a scene from the mid-1960s which might barely see its 50th anniversary if ambitious plans come to pass. There has been considerable recent talk that the Dundee city centre of the 21st century should be 're-introduced' to its historic waterfront. We might, however, have to wait until *Dundee in old picture postcards volume 3* to see whether the plans to remove or realign the landfall roads system, and perhaps even the Tay Bridge itself, come to fruition!

THE TAY ROAD BRIDGE AND TERMINAL, DUNDEE